ROCKY MOUNTAIN

KETTLE

Cuisine

ROCKY MOUNTAIN

KETTLE

Cuisine

DUTCH OVEN COOKERY BY

SHEILA MILLS

BACKEDDY BOOKS

ROCKY MOUNTAIN KETTLE CUISINE

Copyright © 1980 Sheila Mills

All rights reserved

Published by Backeddy Books

ISBN: 0-9604762-0-2

Printed in the United States of America

CONTENTS

PREFACE

All of the recipes in this book are geared to cooking outdoors. They can, however, be easily adapted to indoor cooking. The recipes have been tested at home in a conventional oven as well as outdoors in a Dutch oven.

My interest in creative cooking techniques was inspired by my mother, Jane McDonald, who has never lost her interest and ability to prepare nutritious, excellent food on a day-to-day basis. The other person to whom I give much credit for the interest I developed in Dutch oven cuisine is my husband, David Mills. My initial exposure to Dutch oven cooking happened in the Idaho wilderness one March while we were on a river raft trip. All the cooking was done in a Dutch oven. Besides the delicious recipes I learned about from wilderness river runs, I have to give credit to several friends and relatives who offered an array of diverse cooking ideas and recipes. In addition, I experimented with recipes which seemed appropriate only to kitchen preparation, and found that even fine cuisine can be prepared to perfection in a Dutch oven outdoors.

Rocky Mountain Kettle Cuisine is a compilation of several years of testing and perfection of recipes that I know to be especially delicious outdoors, and a delightful change when cooked at home.

CARE & USE

THE DUTCH OVEN — ITS USE AND CARE

The Dutch oven is a versatile cooking pot that substitutes for a host of outdoor cooking utensils. With its snug-fitting lid in place, and heated with coals from a wood or charcoal fire, it becomes an oven. Food can be baked, braised, stewed, or roasted. With the lid removed, the oven becomes a kettle for boiling, deep-fat frying or heating food quickly over a fire. Even the lid doubles in service and can be converted into a frying pan.

A true camp Dutch oven is easily identified by its legs, which extend below the oven and permit it to sit over hot coals, and its flat lid, which has a vertical lip around the outside edge to retain the hot coals which are placed on top.

There are several types of Dutch ovens on the market. The camp Dutch oven is not regularly stocked by supermarkets and hardware stores, so you may need to order it directly from the manufacturer or a river supply or outdoor equipment catalog. The important thing to watch for when purchasing a Dutch oven for outdoor use is that it is not simply a flat-bottomed kettle made for kitchen cooking, unless, of course, you plan on preparing the recipes which follow only at home in the conventional oven.

The camp Dutch oven is made specifically for open-fire cooking. It is made of heavy cast iron or aluminum in basic sizes from eight inches to sixteen inches in diameter, and from four to six inches deep.

The **cast iron Dutch oven** is heavy, thick, and flat on the bottom with three short legs. The lid is tight fitting and has a vertical lip with a handle in the center. There is also a bail for lifting the entire unit.

Proper seasoning of a cast iron camp Dutch oven is essential. If you scour your oven with strong detergents, it will need reseasoning frequently. Rub the oven with unsalted shortening and place it in your oven at home until it smokes, then wipe out the excess fat. If you are camping just place it on the coals with the lid on until it smokes. Then, wipe it out. If you wash it with detergent between uses, it is a good idea to grease it to keep it from rusting. It is best, too, to store a cast iron Dutch oven upside down and with the lid off.

The **aluminum Dutch oven** is popular with campers because it is lightweight, rustproof, and requires no seasoning. Cast iron, though it is heavier than aluminum and takes longer to heat, heats evenly and stays hot for a long period of time. The aluminum Dutch is one-third the weight of cast iron, and thus it is more portable on camping trips. It is the only model that can be backpacked by a hiker. The two types cost about the same. It is important that you do not overheat an aluminum oven because you can cause permanent damage.

A Dutch oven can be used over a charcoal or wood fire, hardwoods being the best, since they produce a lot of hot coals. If charcoal briquets are used, allow twenty to thirty minutes for them to heat properly before placing them around the oven. A combination of charcoal briquets and wood coals works well and keeps the heat constant. It is a good idea to preheat the lid when baking to prevent heat from being drawn out of the porous iron by cold ingredients.

Most of the following recipes are adapted for six to eight servings and can be prepared in a ten- or twelve-inch oven. An aluminum oven, which I prefer, heats quickly and requires 6 to 8 briquets evenly distributed underneath and 12 to 16 briquets on the lid for a twelve-inch Dutch. Using additional coals to try to speed up the cooking time is unwise, since it can damage the aluminum and cause the food to burn.

Cast iron requires more cooking time than aluminum, but the number of coals on top and bottom remains the same.

The cast iron or aluminum Dutch oven can be permanently damaged by pouring cold water into a hot oven; by uneven heating caused by putting coals on only half the oven or lid; by careless packing while traveling (the legs can be broken off or pushed up through the bottom by too much jamming); by rust and corrosion.

The lid, turned upside down on the coals, can be used for frying. When using more than one oven, the second can be stacked on top of the first and so on, without the necessity of spreading more briquets on the ground.

Judging when a Dutch oven meal is ready is learned from experience. As one boatman puts it, "It falls somewhere between instinct and sense of smell."

When checking for doneness, do not leave the lid off any longer than necessary. It is like opening your oven door at home — you lose all the heat. Turning the oven and the lid a quarter of a turn every ten to fifteen minutes helps it to bake more evenly. It is very important that the lid is tightly sealed. You may lightly tap it with a pair of pliers (an indispensible tool for Dutch oven cooking), but be careful not to cause your leavened foods to fall.

The original camp Dutch oven evolved through centuries of experience. It was designed for cooking complete meals on open fires without the need for other appliances. (A shovel, pliers, and leather gloves come in handy, though.) It is at once a kettle, a frying pan, an oven, a pot, and a stove — all in one portable utensil. A unique cooking device, the Dutch oven can produce delicious and nutritious meals with little trouble or skill.

To demonstrate the talents of the camp Dutch oven I have included a variety of dishes in this cookbook. If you are not acquainted with an authentic camp Dutch oven, I suggest you make friends with one right away. Use your oven to prepare leisurely campsite meals, and then settle back and enjoy some of the most delectable dishes you have ever eaten.

SOUPS

ASPARAGUS AND LEEK CHOWDER
(Serves 6-8)

3 cups	sliced, fresh mushrooms
3	large leeks, sliced
1	10 oz. package frozen cut asparagus, thawed
6 Tbsp.	butter
3 Tbsp.	flour
½ Tsp.	salt
Dash	pepper
2 cups	chicken broth
2 cups	light cream
1 Tbsp.	chopped pimiento
Dash	crushed saffron

In Dutch oven, cook mushrooms, leeks, and asparagus in butter till tender but not browned □ Stir in flour, salt, and pepper □ Add chicken broth and light cream to vegetable mixture; cook and stir till mixture is thickened and bubbly □ Stir in the chopped pimiento and crushed saffron □ Heat through but do not boil.

AVOCADO SOUP
(Serves 4)

1	large ripe avocado, peeled and pitted
2 cups	milk
½ Tsp.	kelp
¼ Tsp.	oregano
	Yogurt

Mash avocado or blend in electric blender □ Gradually beat or blend in milk.

Add kelp and oregano □ Pour into saucepan or Dutch oven and heat until simmering □ Do not boil or the avocado will taste bitter □ Serve hot topped with yogurt.

BROCCOLI CHOWDER
(Serves 4)

1	10 oz. pkg. frozen chopped broccoli or fresh broccoli, chopped till tender
4 cups	medium white sauce (page 72)
2 Tbsp.	butter
4 Tbsp.	green onion, minced
2	beef bouillon cubes, dissolved in ¼ cup boiling water
¼ Tsp.	salt
Dash	pepper
Dash	ground nutmeg

Prepare medium white sauce (see Thundermountain Chicken and Broccoli under **Fish & Poultry**) ☐ Saute onion in butter until tender ☐ Combine all ingredients in Dutch oven and simmer for 15 minutes ☐ Serve hot ☐ (Sprinkle 1 Tbsp. shredded cheddar cheese on top.)

CHEESY ASPARAGUS SOUP
(Serves 4)

This delicious soup is a real tastebud tantalizer!

1	pkg. frozen asparagus, thawed and drained
4 cups	medium white sauce (page 72)
2 cups	cheddar cheese, shredded
¼ cup	bacon bits
½ Tsp.	salt

Prepare white sauce (recipe page 72) ☐ Add cheese and stir till it is melted ☐ Add salt, bacon bits and asparagus and stir constantly for 10 minutes ☐ Serve hot.

CHITTAM CREEK CHILI
(Serves 8)

4 Tbsp.	oil
2	onions, chopped
2	cloves garlic, crushed
2 lbs.	ground beef
1	large green pepper, chopped
2	cans whole tomatoes (14-16 oz.)
2 pt.	water
2	bay leaves
1 Tsp.	chili powder
Pinch	basil
	Salt and pepper to taste
2	cans red kidney beans

Heat oil, add onions, garlic and saute for a few minutes □ Add meat and pepper and cook until brown □ Add all the other ingredients except the beans; bring to a boil and reduce the heat (remove half of the coals) and simmer gently, uncovered, until the sauce thickens, about ½ hour □ Add the beans, correct the seasoning, cover and cook another ½ hour.

CLAM CHOWDER
(Serves 4)

1	can minced clams
1	can whole, baby clams
4 cups	medium white sauce (page 72)
¼ cup	green onions, minced
2 Tbsp.	butter
¼ cup	celery, minced
1 Tsp.	salt

Prepare medium white sauce (recipe page 72) □ Saute onions and celery in butter until tender □ Combine all ingredients and cook, stirring constantly for 10 minutes □ Clam juice may be substituted for some of the milk in the white sauce and added to dilute the soup □ Serve hot.

SOUPS

CREAM OF CELERY SOUP
(Serves 4)

2 cups	chicken stock or broth
6	ribs celery, chopped and sauteed
½	medium onion, thinly sliced
2 Tbsp.	flour
2 Tbsp.	butter
1½ cups	half and half
	Salt

Melt butter, add flour □ Cook 2 minutes □ Gradually add half and half, stirring constantly until sauce thickens □ Add chicken stock □ Saute onion and celery until tender □ Add to mixture and season to taste.

CREAM OF MUSHROOM SOUP
(Serves 4-5)

1 lb.	fresh mushrooms, sliced
3	chicken bouillon cubes, dissolved in 2 cups boiling water
2	green onions, chopped
¼ cup	butter
3 Tbsp.	flour
3 cups	milk
	Salt and pepper
	Chopped parsley
2 Tbsp.	bacon bits

Saute mushrooms and onions in 2 Tbsp. butter □ Melt butter in saucepan and blend in flour □ Gradually add milk and cook, stirring, until slightly thickened □ Add mushrooms and onions to bouillon □ Add white sauce to bouillon and season to taste with salt and pepper □ Sprinkle with parsley □ Serve hot.

MIKE'S BUTTERMILK SOUP

(Serves 6-8) Mike DeLate — Boatman & Birdwatcher

3 Tbsp.	safflower oil
1 cup	millet (cover bottom of Dutch oven)
1 bunch	green onions, chopped
1	lb. mushrooms, sliced and sauteed
2 qts.	buttermilk

Fry millet in oil until it makes your eyes water □ Add onions cooking until dark brown □ Add buttermilk and mushrooms and stir □ Serve hot with green salad and homemade, whole wheat bread.

OYSTER STEW

(Serves 4)

3	cans oysters
4 cups	medium white sauce (page 72)
¼ cup	green onions, chopped
¼ cup	celery, chopped
1 Tsp.	salt
2 Tbsp.	parsley flakes

Prepare white sauce from page 72 □ Use part of the juice from the oysters to take the place of an equal amount of milk □ Saute the onions and celery until tender in 2 Tbsp. butter □ Combine all ingredients and mix well, stirring until hot.

SOUPS

SALMON RIVER STEW
(Serves 8-10)

2 lbs.	beef chuck, cut in 1½-inch cubes
1 lb.	pork sausage, ground
1	clove garlic
3	medium onion, sliced
2	bay leaves
1 Tbsp.	salt
2 Tsp.	pepper
6	carrots, sliced
4	potatoes, cubed
2	green peppers, cubed
6	fresh tomatoes, cubed
½ lb.	cheddar cheese, shredded

Brown beef and sausage □ Drain well □ Add 2 cups hot water and next 9 ingredients □ Cover; simmer for 45-50 minutes, stirring occasionally to keep from sticking □ Remove bay leaves and garlic □ Cook till vegetables are tender another 10 minutes □ Sprinkle cheese on top and put lid back on Dutch oven until cheese melts.

SOUPE A L'OIGNON
(Serves 8)

4	onions, thinly sliced
2 Tbsp.	butter
1 Tbsp.	oil
8 cups	beef bouillon
½ cup	dry white wine
2 Tbsp.	flour
	Salt and pepper to taste
8	1-inch sliced French bread, hard toasted
¼ to ½ lb.	grated Swiss or Parmesan cheese

Cook the onions slowly in butter and oil in covered saucepan or Dutch oven for 30 minutes until deep golden brown, stirring frequently □ Sprinkle with flour and stir for 2-3 minutes □ Away from heat, add bouillon and wine and season to taste □ Simmer 30 minutes partially covered □ Ladle the soup into bowls over the rounds of bread □ Sprinkle with cheese □ (If you're at home, place under broiler until cheese is bubbly and lightly browned.)

ZUCCHINI SOUP
(Serves 6-8)

5	medium-sized zucchini, thinly sliced
¼ cup	butter
1	medium onion, chopped
2 cans	chicken broth
½ cup	light cream
⅛ Tsp.	salt and pepper

Heat butter in Dutch oven and add zucchini and onion and saute until limp □ Add broth, cover and simmer until vegetables are tender □ Pour into a blender (if you're home) and whirl until smooth □ Add cream, salt and pepper □ Serve hot or cold.

SOUPS

BREADS

BARGAMIN BEER BREAD

Vic Bargamin moved from Virginia to Idaho in the 1880s to hunt, trap and prospect. He settled between the Salmon and Clearwater rivers and has a creek named after him in that area.

1½ cups	self-rising flour
1½ cups	whole wheat flour
3 Tbsp.	sugar or honey
1 Tbsp.	salt
1 can	warm beer — your favorite
¼ lb.	butter

Mix dry ingredients together; make well in the center □ Add ⅓ of the beer; stir lightly, add ⅓ more of the beer, stirring lightly; add last of the beer and mix just to moisten dry ingredients □ Melt ¼ lb. butter, pour over top of bread every 15 minutes while baking □ It should double in size □ Bake for 30-35 minutes in Dutch oven or 1 hour in conventional oven at 350°F.

BRAN WHEAT MUFFINS
(Makes 1 dozen)

1 cup	unbleached flour
1 cup	whole wheat flour (unsifted)
¾ cup	whole bran cereal
3 Tsp.	baking powder
½ Tsp.	salt
1	egg
¼ cup	melted butter or oil
4 Tbsp.	honey
1 cup	milk

Combine dry ingredients and mix, forming a well in the center □ Lightly beat the egg; stir in melted butter, honey and milk □ Pour all at once into the well of the flour □ Stir just to moisten ingredients, scraping the bottom of the bowl as you stir □ Batter should look lumpy.

Grease muffin cups or line them with paper baking cups □ In the Dutch oven, line the bottom with paper baking cups, filling each ⅔ full with batter □ Bake at 375°F for about 25 minutes or until well browned □ In the Dutch oven bake for 15-20 minutes □ Serve muffins hot with butter and/or honey.

BREADS

CORN BREAD
(Serves 6)

1¾ cup	yellow corn meal
¼ cup	whole wheat flour
¼ cup	dry milk
3 Tbsp.	baking powder
1 Tsp.	sea salt
1	egg, lightly beaten
1 Tbsp.	honey
2 Tbsp.	butter
1½ cup	milk

Combine corn meal, flour, milk powder, baking powder, and salt □ Add remaining ingredients and stir until moist □ Turn into buttered pan or Dutch oven and bake at 425°F for 20-25 minutes.

DILLY CASSEROLE BREAD

1 pkg.	yeast
¼ cup	warm water
1 cup	creamed cottage cheese
2 Tbsp.	honey
1 Tsp.	instant minced onion
1 Tbsp.	margarine
2 Tsp.	dill weed
1 Tsp.	salt
¼ Tsp.	baking soda
1	unbeaten egg
2¼ to 2½ cups	flour

Soften yeast in water □ Combine in mixing bowl: cottage cheese (lukewarm), honey, onion, margarine, dill weed, salt, soda, egg and yeast □ Add flour and beat well □ Cover □ Let rise until double in size □ Stir down batter □ Turn into 10″ Dutch oven, or casserole, buttered □ Let rise 30-40 minutes □ Bake in Dutch oven 30 to 40 minutes □ Bake at 350°F for 40 to 50 minutes in conventional oven □ Brush with soft butter and sprinkle with salt □ Makes 1 loaf.

KLINKHAMMER COFFEE CAKE
(Serves 10)

Shepp Ranch on the Main Salmon River in Idaho was purchased in the early 1900s by Charlie Shepp and Peter Klinkhammer. Pete spent nearly 50 years on this ranch, selling it in 1950 for $10,000, 10 times what they paid for it.

½ cup	margarine or butter
1¼ cup	brown sugar
2½ cups	wholewheat flour
1 Tbsp.	baking powder
1½ Tsp.	baking soda
¼ Tsp.	salt
3	eggs
1 cup	milk
1 Tsp.	vanilla
1 cup	yogurt

Mix dry ingredients together, making a well in the center; melt the butter, beat the eggs slightly and add to them the milk, vanilla and yogurt □ Pour the liquids in the flour well and mix only to moisten the dry ingredients □ Pour them into a Dutch oven.

Topping:

¼ cup	butter, melted
¾ cup	chopped walnuts
¾ cup	brown sugar
1½ Tsp.	cinnamon
¾ cup	raisins (optional)

Combine above topping ingredients and sprinkle on top of coffee cake batter □ Bake in Dutch oven for 20-25 minutes □ Cool slightly before slicing.

BREADS

DUTCH OVEN CINNAMON ROLLS

Use the recipe for whole wheat bread in this same section □ After the dough has risen the first time, divide it in half □ On lightly floured board roll each in a rectangle to about ¼ inch thick □ Brush each with 1 Tbsp. melted butter.

Combine 1 cup raisins, ½ cup brown sugar or fructose, ½ cup chopped walnuts, and 1 Tsp. ground cinnamon; sprinkle half over each piece of dough □ Roll each as for jelly roll, starting with long edge □ In the bottom of the Dutch oven melt ½ lb. butter, sprinkle on ¼ cup brown sugar □ Cut rolls into 1-inch slices □ Place sealed side down when placing the pieces in the oven □ Cover and let rise till doubled, about ½ hour □ Bake at 375°F for 25 minutes □ Bake in the Dutch oven for 20 minutes or until golden brown.

NO-KNEAD OATMEAL BREAD

Combine:

2 cups	boiling water
1 cup	rolled oats
⅓ cup	shortening
½ cup	light molasses (or honey)
1 Tbsp.	salt

Cool to lukewarm □ Add 2 packages of yeast; mix well □ Blend in 2 eggs □ Add gradually 6½ cups whole wheat flour, mixing until dough is well blended □ Place dough in greased bowl or Dutch oven and cover □ (At this point you may put dough in refrigerator or cold place for several hours) □ Shape dough into 2 loaves on well-floured board and place in greased loaf pans or Dutch oven and cover □ Let rise in warm place until double in bulk, about 2 hours □ Bake in Dutch oven for ¾ hour or in moderate oven (350°) for 1 hour.

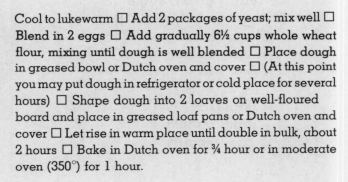

SOURDOUGH WHOLE WHEAT BREAD

To make starter batter: Dissolve 1 package active dry yeast in ½ cup warm water □ Stir in 2 cups lukewarm water, 2 cups flour, 1 teaspoon salt, and 1 tablespoon sugar □ Beat till smooth □ Let stand, uncovered at room temperature 3 to 5 days □ Stir 2 or 3 times daily; cover at night □ (Starter should have "yeasty," not sour, smell) □ Cover, and refrigerate till ready to make bread.

1	pkg. active dry yeast
1½ cups	warm water
1 cup	starter batter
2 Tsp.	salt
2 Tsp.	sugar or honey
5 to 5¼ cups	whole wheat flour
½ Tsp.	soda

To make bread: In large bowl, soften yeast in warm water □ Blend in starter batter, salt and sugar □ Add 3 cups of flour □ Beat 3 to 4 minutes □ Cover; let rise till double (about 2 hours) □ Mix soda with 1½ cups flour; stir into dough □ Add enough additional flour for stiff dough □ Turn out on lightly floured surface; knead 8 to 10 minutes □ Divide dough in half; cover and let rest 10 minutes □ Shape in 2 round or oval loaves □ Place on lightly greased baking sheets □ With sharp knife, make diagonal gashes across top □ Let rise till double (1½ hours) □ Bake at 400°F for 35 to 40 minutes □ Brush with butter □ In the Dutch oven bake for 30 to 35 minutes.

To keep starter: Add ½ cup water, ½ cup flour, and 1 Tsp. sugar to leftover starter □ Let stand till bubbly and well fermented, at least 1 day □ Store in the refrigerator or cooler □ If not used within 10 days, add 1 Tsp. sugar.

BREADS

WHOLE WHEAT BREAD

4	pkg. yeast
1 cup	honey
3½ cups	warm water
1 Tsp.	salt
3 Tbsp.	oil
9 cups	whole wheat flour

In large bowl dissolve yeast in water; add honey and stir until dissolved □ Add oil and salt — stir well □ Add flour one cup at a time, mixing until stiff □ Roll dough out onto floured surface and **knead until smooth and elastic** □ Shape dough into a ball □ Place the dough in oiled bowl and let rise until double in size □ (This may take 2 hours.)

Cut the dough into 2 portions for 2 Dutch ovens or 3 portions for bread pans □ Shape and place in Dutch ovens or pans, well buttered □ Let rise until double in size.

Bake in moderate oven (350°) about 35-40 minutes or in Dutch oven for 25-30 minutes. The bread should be golden brown □ Remove from pans immediately and cool slightly before slicing.

ZUCCHINI BREAD

3	eggs
1 cup	honey
1 cup	salad oil

Mix well □ Add and stir:

3 Tsp.	vanilla
2 cups	washed and grated zucchini (unpeeled)

Add and mix well:

3 cups	whole wheat flour
1 Tsp.	salt
1 Tsp.	cinnamon
1 Tsp.	ginger
1 Tsp.	baking soda
¼ Tsp.	baking powder
1 cup	chopped walnuts

Pour into greased and floured 10″ Dutch oven or 2 loaf pans □ Bake in Dutch oven about 1 hour, turning Dutch oven every 15 minutes, or at 325°F in conventional oven for 1 hour until knife inserted in center comes out clean □ Remove from pan and let cool before slicing.

MEATLESS DISHES

ASPARAGUS AND CHEESE SANDWICHES

1	pkg. whole wheat English muffins, halved
1	pkg. frozen asparagus spears, thawed and drained
1 lb.	swiss cheese, shredded or sliced
1	can pitted black olives, sliced
1	pkg. premixed, dry Hollandaise sauce, or Jiffy Hollandaise (see recipe below)
	paprika

Brown muffins in Dutch oven or under broiler □ Arrange asparagus, olives, and cheese on muffins □ Bake from top and bottom in Dutch or put under broiler in oven until cheese melts □ Pour Hollandaise sauce on each and garnish with paprika.

Jiffy Hollandaise: Combine ¼ cup sour cream, ¼ cup mayonnaise, ½ Tsp. mustard, and 1 Tsp. lemon juice □ Cook and stir over low heat till heated through.

BAKED RICE
(Serves 4-6) A Steven Shephard recipe.

1 cup	long-grained rice
2½ cups	water

Blend with hot water:

2	bouillon cubes (any flavor)
2 Tsp.	minced garlic
½ cup	chopped celery
½ cup	sliced mushrooms
	salt and pepper

When almost done stir in 1 cup grated cheddar cheese and recover until done.

Bake with coals top and bottom for about 1 hour.

BRUSSELS SPROUTS QUICHE
(Serves 6-8)

	Pastry for 10-inch pie shell
10-12 oz.	fresh Brussels sprouts
	Lightly salted boiling water
½ cup	slivered almonds
2	eggs
½ cup	milk
½ cup	mayonnaise
2 cups	Swiss or cheddar cheese, shredded
⅛ Tsp.	pepper
⅛ Tsp.	ground nutmeg

Prepare pastry using your favorite recipe or a mix □ Line the bottom of the Dutch oven or pie pan □ Trim off stem ends of brussel sprouts, rinse thoroughly, then cut into quarters □ Cook in a large quantity of lightly salted boiling water until just tender, about 4 to 5 minutes □ Drain, plunge into cold water to cool quickly, and drain on paper towels □ Spread almonds on a shallow baking pan and toast in a 350° oven for 8 minutes or until golden □ (This can be done in the Dutch oven, also) □ Place Brussels sprouts in the bottom of the pastry shell and sprinkle with toasted almonds.

Mix together the eggs, milk, mayonnaise, cheese, pepper, and nutmeg; blend until smooth □ Pour over Brussels sprouts and nuts in the pie shell □ Sprinkle top with ¾ cup of the cheese.

Bake at 350° for 30-35 minutes or until the custard is firm in the center, or in a Dutch oven for 25-30 minutes.

Allow to stand about 10 minutes before serving.

CHEESE "SOUFFLE" CASSEROLE
(Serves 6)

8 slices	bread, crust removed
8 oz.	cheddar or Swiss cheese, grated
1 cup	cooked and chopped meat or shrimp (optional)
4	eggs
1 cup	light cream or milk
1 cup	evaporated milk
¼ Tsp.	salt
1 Tbsp.	parsley
	Paprika

Alternate layers of bread and cheese and, if desired, meat in Dutch oven or casserole □ Beat together eggs, milk, salt and parsley □ Pour over bread and cheese □ Sprinkle top with paprika □ Bake 40-45 minutes.

CHEF'S HATS
(Serves 6)

1	pkg. frozen pattie shells
1½ cups	cheddar cheese, shredded
3 Tbsp.	flour
3	eggs, slightly beaten
1	10-oz. pkg. frozen spinach, thawed and drained
¼ lb.	fresh mushrooms, sliced
6	crisply cooked bacon slices, crumbled
½ Tsp.	salt
Dash	pepper

Roll out each pattie shell into a 6-8 inch circle □ Line muffin cups or individual aluminum cups with each circle of dough, so that the edges stand up at least a half-inch above the cup edge.

Toss cheese with flour, add remaining ingredients; mix well □ Fill the cups with cheese mixture □ Bake in 350°F oven for 40 minutes or in a Dutch oven for 25-30 minutes.

MEATLESS DISHES

DAISY TAPPAN RICE DISH
(Serves 10-12)

This recipe was given to me by my mother and renamed for Daisy Tappan, who came to the Middle Fork of the Salmon River to live when she was a child of seven. She was every bit as competent in the back country as any man who ever lived there and spent most of her 70 years there, ranching and raising her family.

2 cups	brown rice
½ cup	butter
1 cup	olives, black pitted, chopped
2 cans	chicken broth or beef broth
1 cup	cheddar cheese, shredded
2	fresh tomatoes, chopped
3 Tbsp.	chopped onions
¾ cup	green pepper, chopped
1 cup	water

Combine all of the above ingredients and mix well □ Bake at 325° for 1½ hours in a conventional oven or in the Dutch oven for 55-60 minutes.

EGGS ELEGANT
(Serves 6-8)

½ Tsp.	salt
¼ Tsp.	pepper
1 Tbsp.	dry mustard
2 cans	cream of chicken soup
1 cup	milk
2 cups	cheddar cheese, grated
1	package asparagus pieces, thawed & drained
6-8	eggs
	Paprika as garnish
4	whole wheat English muffins

Combine first 5 ingredients in Dutch oven □ Stir over medium heat until smooth and creamy □ Stir in cheese until melted □ Add asparagus pieces □ Make hollows for 6-8 eggs and break an egg into each one □ Bake 15-20 minutes or until eggs are set to your liking □ Serve over muffins.

EGGPLANT QUICHE
(Serves 6)

1	10-inch pastry shell
1	small eggplant
2	tomatoes, peeled, seeded, chopped, drained
½ cup	chopped onion
¼ cup	olive oil
1	clove garlic, minced
¼ cup	sliced ripe olives
½ Tsp.	dried oregano leaves, crumbled
¼ Tsp.	freshly ground pepper
	Salt
4	eggs
1½ cups	whipping cream
½ cup	grated Parmesan cheese

Line bottom of Dutch oven with pastry.

Heat oven to 350°F if using a conventional □ Bake eggplant in Dutch oven or oiled baking pan until tender when pierced with fork, 35-40 minutes; cool slightly □ Remove and discard skin; chop eggplant coarsely □ Combine eggplant and tomatoes in colander; press mixture gently; drain 15 minutes.

Increase heat to 425°F □ Saute onion in oil until soft, about 5 minutes □ Add eggplant mixture and garlic; saute 2 minutes □ Stir in olives, oregano and pepper □ Season to taste with salt □ Drain mixture in colander 2 to 3 minutes.

Spread eggplant mixture over bottom of pastry shell □ Beat eggs in small bowl; beat in cream, pour over eggplant mixture □ Sprinkle with cheese □ Bake 15 minutes; remove half of the coals □ Bake until knife inserted halfway between edge and center of quiche is withdrawn clean; about 30 minutes □ Serve hot or cold.

GREEN RICE CASSEROLE
(Serves 8-10)

1⅓ cups	evaporated milk
½ cup	cooking oil
3	eggs
¼	small onion, minced
½	small carrot, minced
2 cups	fresh parsley leaves, minced, or 1 10-oz. package frozen chopped spinach, thawed and drained
2 Tsp.	salt
¼ Tsp.	pepper
1 cup	shredded sharp cheese
3 cups	cooked long-grain rice

Beat milk, oil and eggs together until well combined □ Add all remaining ingredients; mix well □ Pour into greased Dutch oven □ Bake 1 hour □ In conventional oven, bake at 350°F 1 hour.

GRILLED CHEESE WITH AVOCADO SANDWICHES
(Serves 4)

8	slices whole wheat bread
4 Tbsp.	butter
2	ripe avocados, sliced
1	3-oz. pkg. cream cheese
4	slices cheddar cheese

Butter bread □ Use lid of Dutch oven or bottom of oven to grill □ Layer cheese, avocados, cream cheese on bread □ Cook till golden brown and cheese is melted □ Cut sandwiches in half and serve □ Broil in conventional oven.

GRILLED CREAM CHEESE AND OLIVE SANDWICHES
(Serves 4)

8	slices whole wheat bread
4 Tbsp.	butter
1	can pitted, black olives, sliced
1	8-oz. pkg. cream cheese

Grill on the top of the Dutch oven lid or in the bottom of the Dutch □ Butter all slices of bread □ Spread cream cheese generously on each slice and top with olives □ Grill until golden brown and cheese is soft □ In conventional oven use broiler or grill on stove top.

OAKIE'S EGGPLANT CASSEROLE
(Serves 4-6)

2	eggplants, sliced very thinly with skin on
	Salt and pepper
	Flour
½ cup	olive oil
2 cups	tomato sauce
½ lb.	**Mozzarella cheese, grated** Parmesan cheese

Flour, salt and pepper eggplant slices □ Brown in oil □ Pour ⅓ cup tomato sauce on bottom of Dutch oven □ Arrange alternate layers □ Sprinkle top with Parmesan cheese □ (Bacon bits can be added) □ Bake uncovered in a 350°F oven for 40 minutes or in the Dutch oven with coals top and bottom for 30 minutes.

SKOOKUMCHUCK SCRAMBLED EGGS
(Serves 10-12)

2	dozen eggs, well beaten
⅓	bunch green onions, minced
¼ cup	bacon bits
2 Tbsp.	flaked parsley
¼	green pepper, minced
½ lb.	cheddar cheese, shredded
¼ cup	milk

Saute onions and pepper in 2 Tbsp. butter until tender □ Add eggs, bacon bits, and parsley and mix well □ Stir frequently until eggs are cooked □ Add milk and cheese and stir until cheese melts □ Serve immediately.

SUPER NUT BURGERS
(Makes about a dozen)

Here is another great high protein, meatless meal from my sister, Marcia Colliat □ Surprise your family and friends with this one and have them guess what kind of meat is in it — nut meat!

1 cup	almonds
1 cup	sunflower seeds
1 cup	cashews
1 cup	walnuts
1 cup	fine celery
1 cup	carrot pulp (takes 3-4 carrots)
1 cup	fresh onion

For your convenience, mix the above in a food processor before leaving home, if you are going to use this recipe camping.

Place the following in a mixing bowl with the above:

½ cup	whey powder
2	eggs
1 Tsp.	poultry seasoning
¼ Tsp.	dry mustard
½ Tsp.	garlic powder or fresh clove pressed
¼ Tsp.	sage
1 Tsp.	cumin
1 Tsp.	chili powder
¼ Tsp.	curry powder
1 Tsp.	dry parsley

Mix well and form into small patties □ Fry on lid or inside Dutch oven.

TASTY TOMATO DRESSING

This is great on the nut burgers or a salad.

⅓ cup	lemon juice
1 cup	oil
1 Tsp.	protein powder
1 Tsp.	tomari
1-2	cloves garlic
½	onion

Place the above in a blender and blend well before leaving home ☐ Add cut up: 2 tomatoes, 1 bell pepper, 2-3 stalks of celery.

It makes a delicious, chunky sauce.

VEGETARIAN LASAGNA

10	lasagna noodles
1 lb.	fresh spinach
2 cups	sliced mushrooms
1 cup	grated carrot
½ cup	chopped onion
1 Tbsp.	oil
1	15-oz. can tomato sauce
1	6-oz. can tomato paste
½ cup	chopped pitted ripe olives
1½ Tsp.	dried oregano, crushed
2 cups	cottage cheese
16 oz.	Monterey Jack cheese, sliced
	Grated Parmesan cheese

Cook lasagna noodles in boiling unsalted water for 8 to 10 minutes or till tender; drain ☐ Rinse spinach well ☐ In saucepan, cook spinach covered, without water except for the drops that cling to leaves ☐ Reduce heat when steam forms ☐ Cook 3 to 5 minutes, turning occasionally ☐ In saucepan cook mushrooms, carrot, and onion in hot oil till tender but not brown ☐ Stir in tomato sauce, tomato paste, olives and oregano ☐ In Dutch oven or greased baking dish, layer half each of the noodles, cottage cheese, spinach, jack cheese, and sauce mixture; repeat layers, reserving several cheese slices for the top ☐ Bake in 375°F oven for 30 minutes or in Dutch oven with coals on top and bottom for 30 minutes ☐ Let stand 10 minutes before serving ☐ Sprinkle each serving with Parmesan.

WALNUT PECAN RING
(Serves 4-6)

This recipe was given to me by my sister, Marcia Colliat, who has collected many delicious high-protein, meatless main dishes.

3	eggs
2	medium stalks of celery, sliced
1	large carrot, grated
½	medium onion, grated
1 cup	chopped walnuts
1 cup	chopped pecans
1½ cups	bread crumbs
1½ cups	yogurt
2 Tbsp.	soy sauce
1 Tbsp.	kelp
2 T.	chopped fresh parsley

Beat eggs □ Mix together all ingredients very well and pour into greased 2-quart baking dish and bake at 350°F for one hour or in the Dutch oven with heat on top and bottom for 45 minutes.

ZUCCHINI ENCHILADAS
(Serves 6-8)

1	pkg. flour tortillas
4	medium-sized zucchini, washed and shredded
1 pt.	sour cream
1	bunch green onions, diced
1	8-oz. can tomato sauce
1	small can diced green chiles
1	can pitted black olives, chopped
1 lb.	jack cheese, shredded
½ lb.	cheddar cheese, shredded
2 Tbsp.	cumin
	Salt to taste

Saute onions in 2 Tbsp. butter in Dutch oven □ Mix together onions, zucchini, chiles, olives, cumin, salt and sour cream □ Fill each tortilla with zucchini mixture and roll up, placing in Dutch oven loose edge down □ Pour tomato sauce over all and sprinkle cheese on top □ Bake 30-35 minutes □ Let stand 10 minutes before serving.

BEEF & PORK

BOEUF BOURGUIGNONNE
(Serves 6-8)

6	strips bacon cut in ½-inch pieces
3 lbs.	beef rump or chuck, cut in 1½-inch cubes
1	large carrot, peeled and sliced
1	medium onion, sliced
3 Tbsp.	flour
1	10 oz. can condensed beef broth
1½ cups	red wine
1 Tsp.	tomato paste
	cloves garlic, minced
1½ Tsp.	whole thyme
1	whole bay leaf
½ lb.	white onions, peeled
1 lb.	fresh mushrooms, sliced

Cook bacon in Dutch oven until crisp □ Remove and drain □ Add beef cubes and brown well □ Place browned beef cubes to the side □ Brown carrot and onion □ Season with 1½ Tsp. salt and ⅛ Tsp. pepper; stir in flour □ Add broth, mix well □ Put beef cubes back in Dutch oven □ Add cooked bacon, wine, tomato paste, garlic, bay leaf, and onions □ Cover and bake for 1 hour on medium heat □ Saute mushrooms in 2 Tbsp. margarine and add to Dutch oven 15 minutes before it is done.

EGGS BENEDICT

For each serving, split and toast an English muffin; top with a thin slice of broiled ham or Canadian bacon □ Place a poached egg on the ham □ Prepare a Hollandaise sauce as below, or use the dry mix instant Hollandaise sauce and pour over all □ Sprinkle with paprika and serve immediately.

(The muffins may be toasted in the Dutch oven; the eggs may be poached in the Dutch oven; and the sauce may be prepared in the Dutch oven.)

Hollandaise Sauce Jiffy: Combine ¼ cup dairy sour cream, ¼ cup mayonnaise, ½ Tsp. prepared mustard, and 1 Tsp. lemon juice □ Cook and stir over low heat till heated through □ Makes ½ cup sauce.

CLAIR'S DUTCH OVEN ENCHILADAS
(Serves 6-8)

Clair Yost, who gave me this special recipe, has been boating for fun and commercially for a number of years, and has a special knack for cooking in a Dutch oven, as well as rowing a raft.

1 dozen	corn tortillas
2 lb.	ground beef
2 lb.	sharp cheddar cheese, grated
3	fresh tomatoes, cut into 8 sections each
1	onion, diced
10	fresh mushrooms, sliced
1	green bell pepper, diced
1	medium ripe avocado, diced
1	head lettuce
1	29 oz. can tomato sauce
1	12 oz. can tomato paste
1	10 oz. can enchilada sauce (medium)
	Ground cumin
	Seasoned salt
	Pepper

Brown the beef with diced onion and green pepper □ Season with seasoned salt, 1½ Tbsp. of cumin pepper □ Pour off grease after browning □ In separate Dutch oven heat tomato sauce, paste and enchilada sauce, adding 4 Tbsp. cumin (the key to the dish) and simmer.

Dip each tortilla into the heated sauce to make it soft □ Lay the tortilla on a plate, spread hamburger across the middle of the tortilla □ Put several mushrooms, avocado and 2 sections of tomatoes and grated cheese on top of the beef □ Roll and place in Dutch oven, fold side down □ Put 6 enchiladas (using a 12" Dutch oven) on the first layer □ Pour some sauce over top and spread cheese over that □ Repeat process □ Put remaining hamburger and vegetables and cheese on the top.

Line the outside of the lid with charcoal briquets and 4 in the center □ Place 8 briquets on the bottom □ Bake 30 minutes, checking center and making sure the heat is not too hot □ Bake 15 to 20 minutes more; take coals off and let stand 10 minutes before serving.

Serve enchiladas on top of lettuce leaves □ Top with sour cream and hot sauce.

Variations: Ground beef may be replaced with round steak, chopped and browned □ Beef may be replaced with brown rice and held together with Mozzarella cheese and seasoned with cumin □ Enchilada pie may be made either with the same ingredients, or with four layers, using 3 tortillas cut into fourths to start each layer □ Bake the same way in the Dutch oven.

FANCY EGG SCRAMBLE
(Serves 8-10)

1 cup	diced Canadian bacon
⅓ cup	chopped green onion
3 Tbsp.	butter
12	beaten eggs
¼ lb.	fresh mushrooms
1	recipe Cheese Sauce*
4 Tsp.	butter, melted
2¼ cups	soft bread crumbs (3 slices bread)
⅛ Tsp.	paprika

Prepare cheese sauce first.

In Dutch oven cook Canadian bacon and onion in 3 Tbsp. butter till onion is tender but not brown □ Add eggs and scramble just till set □ Fold mushrooms and eggs into Cheese Sauce □ Combine remaining melted butter, crumbs, and paprika; sprinkle atop eggs □ Cover and bake for 15 minutes □ Remove top coals and bake slowly from bottom another 10 minutes.

***Cheese Sauce:** Melt 2 Tbsp. butter; blend in 2 Tbsp. flour, ½ Tsp. salt, and ⅛ Tsp. pepper □ Add 2 cups milk; cook and stir till bubbly □ Stir in 1 cup shredded cheddar cheese till melted.

FONDUE BREAKFAST
(Serves 6-8)

This delicious breakfast dish recipe was given to me by my aunt, Mac Oliver, from Billings, Montana, where she serves it every year for Christmas Brunch.

6	slices whole wheat bread, cubed
1½ cups	sharp cheddar cheese, grated
⅓ lb.	link sausage (or bulk)
3	eggs
1⅔ cups	milk
½ Tsp.	dry mustard
¼ can	mushroom soup
⅓ cup	milk

Cube bread into Dutch oven or large buttered casserole □ Sprinkle with cheese □ Brown the sausage, drain and cut into thirds □ Place over cheese □ Beat eggs slightly with milk and mustard □ Pour over all □ Refrigerate over night, unless you are camping □ Dilute soup with ⅓ cup milk and pour over all in the morning □ Bake in Dutch oven for about 1 hour, or until it sets up □ Bake at 300°F for 1½ hours in conventional oven.

NICKY'S LASAGNA
(Serves 6-8)

Bill Caccia gave me this recipe, which we made part of the menu on our Main Salmon River float trips. Nicky Holmes gave the recipe to Bill.

1 lb.	ground beef
1	onion, minced
1½ qt.	cottage cheese
1	pkg. lasagna noodles, uncooked
1	large can tomato sauce
1	small can tomato paste
1 lb.	Mozzarella cheese
½ lb.	mushrooms, sliced
½ cup	red wine
	Sweet basil
	Oregano
	Parmesan cheese, grated

Brown the ground beef and onion □ Place half in bottom of Dutch oven □ Spread ½ of cottage cheese on beef □ Cover with ½ package lasagna noodles □ Cover noodles with ½ tomato sauce and paste □ Sprinkle with sweet basil and oregano and ½ cup wine □ Repeat the layer □ Bake 30-35 minutes and add a layer of Mozzarella cheese, covering it with the mushrooms □ Bake 10 minutes more □ Serve with Parmesan cheese and gallons of wine.

Zucchini can be substituted for the beef for vegetarian diets, or used in addition to the beef.

PORK'S COMPANION
(Serves 6-8)

This is a favorite recipe of my good friend, Jim Mulick, who has been floating rivers with us for years. Jim's meat loaf is as spicy as his personality, and he feels the secret ingredient is the pork.

1½ lbs.	ground beef
½ lb.	ground pork
2	beaten eggs
½ cup	wheat germ
½ cup	bread cubes
1	8 oz. can tomato sauce
¼ cup	finely chopped onion
¼ cup	chopped green pepper
¼ cup	chopped celery
1 Tbsp.	Worcestershire sauce
Dash	dried thyme, crushed
½ Tsp.	oregano
½ Tsp.	sage
1 Tsp.	salt

Combine all ingredients; mix well □ Shape mixture into a loaf in the Dutch oven or baking dish □ Bake at 350°F about 1¼ hours or in the Dutch oven for 1 hour, moderately.

PORK CHOPS WITH SPINACH DUMPLINGS
(Serves 6)

6	rib, sirloin, or blade pork chops
	Salt and pepper
½ cup	chopped onion
1	clove garlic, minced
2 cups	tomato juice
1	4 oz. can mushroom stems and pieces, drained
1 Tsp.	sugar
½ Tsp.	salt
Dash	pepper
¼ Tsp.	dried thyme, crushed
¼ Tsp.	dried rosemary, crushed
1	beaten egg
1	10 oz. pkg. frozen chopped spinach, thawed and drained
⅓ cup	fine dry bread crumbs or wheat germ
¼ cup	grated Parmesan cheese
1 Tbsp.	butter, melted
2 Tbsp.	flour

Trim excess fat from chops □ Cook fat trimmings till 2 Tbsp. drippings accumulate □ Discard fat □ Season chops with salt and pepper; brown in hot drippings □ Remove chops; set aside □ In same Dutch oven or skillet, cook onion and garlic till onion is tender but not brown □ Add 1¾ cups of the tomato juice, mushrooms, sugar, salt, pepper, thyme, marjoram and rosemary □ Return chops to skillet □ Simmer, covered, 20-25 minutes □ Meanwhile, combine egg, spinach, bread crumbs, Parmesan, and butter; place 2 Tbsp. of spinach mixture atop each chop to form dumpling □ Simmer, covered, till dumplings are heated through, 10-15 minutes □ Remove chops and dumplings to platter □ Blend flour with the remaining ¼ cup tomato juice □ Stir into pan juices □ Cook and stir till thickened and bubbly □ Serve over chops.

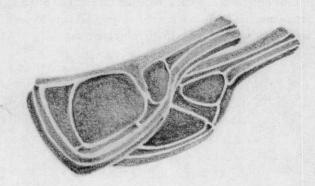

SAUSAGE-STUFFED ACORN SQUASH
(Serves 4-6)

2	large acorn squash, halved
1 lb.	bulk pork sausage
1 cup	chopped celery
½ cup	sliced fresh mushrooms
¼ cup	chopped onion
1	slightly beaten egg
½ cup	dairy sour cream
¼ cup	grated Parmesan cheese
¼ Tsp.	salt

Scoop the seeds out of the 4 halves of squash □ Lightly salt inside of squash □ Place squash in Dutch oven and bake until tender, about 25-30 minutes □ Combine sausage, celery, mushrooms, and onion; cook till vegetables are tender and meat is brown □ Drain well □ Combine egg, sour cream, Parmesan and salt □ Stir into sausage mixture □ Turn squash scooped end up; fill with sausage mixture □ Bake 15-20 minutes more.

STUFFED PORK CHOPS
(Serves 6)

¼ cup	margarine
6	fresh mushrooms, sliced
½ cup	sliced green onions
¾ cup	cooked brown rice
1 Tbsp.	soy sauce
¼ Tsp.	ground ginger
6	large pork chops, 1-inch thick
3 Tbsp.	flour
¼ Tsp.	garlic salt and dry mustard
	Pepper
1	egg, slightly beaten
⅓ cup	fine bread crumbs

Melt 1 Tbsp. margarine □ Add the mushrooms and cook until tender □ Add the onion and rice; stir in soy sauce and ginger □ Remove from heat.

Trim the fat from pork chops and cut a pocket in each □ Stuff with about 3 Tbsp. of the filling □ Secure pockets with skewers or toothpicks.

Combine the flour, garlic salt, mustard and pepper □ Dredge each chop in the flour mixture to coat all sides then dip in egg; drain and dip in crumbs.

Melt the rest of the margarine □ Add the chops and fry slowly, uncovered, until brown on all sides, about 40-45 minutes.

SWEET STEAK
(Serves 6)

My aunt, Mac Oliver, gave me this recipe, which she usually serves with buttered noodles. This recipe was a winner about ten years ago in a Montana Cowbelles beef cook-off.

2 lbs. round steak, cut in serving-sized pieces □ Dredge with flour, pound, and brown in oil □ Salt and pepper to taste.

Make sauce of:

½ cup	minced onion
1 cup	brown sugar
1	7¾ oz. can tomato sauce
1	10½ oz. can pizza sauce
2 cups	water
2 Tbsp.	parsley flakes

Pour sauce over steak in Dutch oven and simmer slowly for about 1½ hours □ Add thickening to gravy if necessary.

WITCHES' BREW
(Serves 8-10)

This is a recipe my mother gave me that has been around for years.

1 lb.	bacon
1 lb.	hamburger
1 cup	diced celery
1 cup	diced onion
1	large can tomatoes
2	cans red kidney beans
1	can mushrooms
1 cup	egg noodles

Fry bacon and hamburger □ Add the onion, celery, tomatoes, beans and mushrooms □ Bake ¾ hour in Dutch oven and 1 hour at 350° for conventional oven.

TAMALE PIE
(Serves 6)

This recipe was given to me by my aunt, Mac Oliver. As she says, there are many recipes for Tamale Pie, all similar, but this has one major difference: the use of Armour Star Tamales, instead of the usual cornmeal crust. It is also good served cold (leftovers) on lettuce leaves, similar to a taco salad.

Saute in 2 Tbsp. oil:

1	medium-size onion, chopped
1	clove garlic (optional), minced (cook until limp, not browned)

Add, and cook to brown:

1 lb.	lean ground beef
½ lb.	bulk pork sausage (discard excess fat)

Add:

1	28 oz. can tomatoes
1	1 lb. can whole kernel corn, drained
1 Tbsp.	chili powder
½ Tsp.	cumin
½ Tsp.	oregano (cover and simmer 10 minutes)

Add:

1 cup	pitted ripe olives, drained (these may be whole or sliced)
1	small can tomato sauce
2	jars of Armour Star Tamales, with corn husks removed, and cut into one- or two-inch chunks. These may be gently stirred into the mixture, with quite a few left on top for appearance.

Sprinkle the top with grated cheddar cheese; about one cup □ Cook until bubbly, and the flavors are melted □ It should be quite a thick consistency □ Cook about 45 minutes.

VEGETABLES

ASPARAGUS SOUFFLE
(Serves 4-6)

3 Tbsp.	butter or margarine
3 Tbsp.	flour
	Salt and pepper
Dash	nutmeg
¼ Tsp.	basil
1 cup	milk
3	eggs, separated
3 Tbsp.	grated Parmesan cheese
1 cup	finely chopped cooked asparagus

Melt butter and blend in flour and seasonings □ Gradually add milk and cook, stirring, until thickened □ Stir in beaten egg yolks □ Remove from heat and add cheese and asparagus □ Fold in stiffly beaten egg whites and turn into well-buttered 1½-quart casserole or Dutch oven □ Bake in moderate oven (375°F) about 45 minutes or in the Dutch oven for 30-35 minutes.

BAKED POTATOES

This recipe was given to me by Steven Shephard, who has been a river guide for 10 years in most of the western states and has cooked in the blazing sun as well as freezing snow. He has nursed slow D.O.'s into the dark, and trimmed burned tops and bottoms off many a cake. His philosophical statement on Dutch ovens is: "You snooze — you lose."

Clean skins and slice off the ends □ Rub with oil (lightly) □ Place disc-shaped flat pebbles in the bottom of the Dutch oven □ Add a little water and place potatoes on the pebbles □ Cover and place hot coals under and on lid of Dutch oven □ For larger amounts terrace ovens on top of one another □ Baking time — 1 hour.

VEGETABLES

BROCCOLI SOUFFLE
(Serves 6)

3 Tbsp.	butter or margarine
3 Tbsp.	flour
	Salt and pepper
Dash	nutmeg
¼ Tsp.	basil
1 cup	milk
3	eggs, separated
¼ cup	Swiss cheese, shredded (cheddar may be used)
1 cup	finely chopped, cooked broccoli

Melt butter and blend in flour and seasonings □ Gradually add milk and cook, stirring, until thickened □ Stir in beaten egg yolks □ Remove from heat and add cheese and broccoli □ Fold in stiffly beaten egg whites and turn into well-buttered Dutch oven or 1½-qt. souffle dish □ Bake in moderate oven (375°) about 45 minutes or in the Dutch oven for 30-35 minutes.

CRAB-STUFFED MUSHROOMS
(Serves 6)

12	large mushrooms
2 Tbsp.	minced green onion (use part of green top)
5 Tbsp.	butter
1 Tsp.	lemon juice
1 cup	flaked, cooked crab meat
½ cup	wheat germ
½ cup	sour cream
¾ cup	shredded Swiss cheese
¼ cup	dry white wine
	Lemon wedges

Wipe mushrooms with a damp cloth; remove the stems and finely chop them □ Saute mushroom stems and onion in 2 Tbsp. butter until onion is limp □ Remove from heat and stir in lemon juice, crab, wheat germ, sour cream and ¼ cup cheese.

Melt remaining 3 Tbsp. butter in Dutch oven □ Turn mushroom caps in the butter to coat □ Spoon about 2 Tbsp. filling in each large cap □ Place mushrooms, filled side up, in Dutch oven □ Before baking, sprinkle mushrooms with remaining cheese and pour wine into Dutch oven □ Bake for 10 to 15 minutes □ Serve hot with lemon wedges.

DUTCH OVEN VEGETABLES
(Serves 6-8) A Steven Shephard recipe.

Slice about 5 cups of vegetables: zucchini, broccoli, cauliflower □ Chop one onion (red or white) and 1 clove garlic □ Grate 1½ cups equally of cheddar and Monterey jack cheese □ Blend Italian seasonings and salt and pepper □ Blend onion, garlic, spices, and cheese with 2 beaten eggs □ Butter bottom and sides of Dutch oven and pour ingredients over vegetables □ Sprinkle some of the cheese on top □ Bake 45 minutes; check for dry knife blade; put coals on top and bottom.

MUSHROOMS AU GRATIN
(Serves 4)

1 lb.	fresh mushrooms
2 Tbsp.	butter
⅓ cup	sour cream
¼ Tsp.	salt
Dash	pepper
1 Tbsp.	flour
¼ cup	chopped parsley
½ cup	shredded Swiss or mild cheddar cheese

Slice mushrooms lengthwise in ¼-inch pieces □ Heat butter over medium heat and saute mushrooms □ Cover Dutch oven for about 2 minutes until they exude juices □ Blend sour cream with salt, pepper and flour until smooth □ Stir into mushroom mixture in pan and heat, stirring until blended and beginning to boil □ Sprinkle parsley and cheese over top and heat until cheese melts, about 10 minutes.

VEGETABLES

SPINACH SOUFFLE
(Serves 6)

My good friend, Mary Jo Mulick, loaned me this recipe several years ago, and it has become a favorite of river runners and Dutch oven cooks.

1	10-oz. package frozen, chopped spinach, thawed and drained
1 cup	cream-style cottage cheese
1 cup	shredded Swiss cheese
3	eggs, beaten well
2 Tbsp.	flour
½ Tsp.	salt
¼ cup	bacon bits

Mix all ingredients together well and pour into Dutch oven or casserole dish □ Bake for 15-20 minutes in Dutch oven, until light and fluffy □ Bake at 350°F in conventional oven for 30-35 minutes.

SQUASH PUFF
(Serves 6)

3 cups	mashed, cooked acorn squash
½ cup	molasses
3 Tbsp.	whole wheat flour
1¼ Tsp.	salt
¼ Tsp.	nutmeg
¼ Tsp.	ginger
3	eggs, separated
¼ cup	finely chopped pecans or walnuts

Blend squash, molasses, flour, salt, nutmeg, ginger and egg yolks □ Beat egg whites until stiff □ Fold into squash mixture □ Turn into Dutch oven or baking dish □ Sprinkle nuts around outside edge and bake 1 hour or until golden brown.

SQUASH SOUFFLE
(Serves 8-10)

3 cups	mashed, cooked winter squash
4 Tbsp.	butter
2 Tbsp.	brown sugar
½ Tsp.	salt
½ Tsp.	grated orange peel
⅛ Tsp.	ground nutmeg
Dash	pepper
4	egg yolks
4	egg whites

In large mixing bowl, combine the squash, butter, brown sugar, salt, orange peel, nutmeg, and pepper □ Beat till fluffy □ Add egg yolks; beat well □ Beat egg whites till stiff peaks form; carefully fold in squash mixture □ Turn into Dutch oven or souffle dish □ Bake in 350°F oven for 55 to 60 minutes or in Dutch oven for 40-45 minutes.

VEGETABLE EGG CUPS
(Serves 6)

1	pkg. frozen pattie shells
1½ cups	cheddar cheese, shredded
3 Tbsp.	flour
3	eggs, slightly beaten
¼ cup	fresh mushrooms, chopped
¼ cup	zucchini, chopped
3 Tbsp.	onion, chopped
6	crisply cooked bacon slices, crumbled
½ Tsp.	salt
Dash	pepper

Roll out each pattie shell into a 6-8 inch circle □ Line muffin cups or use individual aluminum cups with each circle of dough, so that the edges stand up at least a half inch above the cup edge □ Toss cheese with flour, add remaining ingredients; mix well □ Fill the cups with cheese mixture □ Bake in 350°F oven for 50 minutes or in a Dutch oven for 35-40 minutes □ Delicious served for breakfast or a brunch.

VEGETABLES

VEGETABLE SAUTE
(Serves 6)

1	bunch of fresh broccoli, cut up
¼ lb.	fresh mushrooms, sliced
2	medium-sized zucchini, sliced
1	medium onion, sliced
¼ lb.	butter
	Parmesan cheese

Melt butter in Dutch oven □ Add all ingredients and toss together coating it with butter □ Stir fry it until vegetables are still slightly crisp □ Sprinkle with cheese and serve.

WHITIE COX VEGETABLE DISH
(Serves 6-8)

My mother gave me this recipe, which has been a favorite on float trips for years. It was renamed on the Middle Fork of the Salmon River at a campsite named after Whitie Cox, who was killed while placer mining there.

2	10-oz. pkg. Brussels sprouts (frozen)
2	10 oz. pkg. broccoli
1	10 oz. pkg. cauliflower
1	10 oz. pkg. carrots
1	lg. jar Cheez Whiz®
1 can	cream of mushroom soup
½ cup	chopped green onions

Drain vegetables well □ (Fresh vegetables and natural cheddar cheese can be substituted) □ Mix all ingredients in Dutch oven and bake 25-30 minutes.

ZUCCHINI BOATS
(Serves 6)

3	medium-sized zucchini
2	eggs, well beaten
1½ cups	cheddar cheese, shredded
½ cup	cottage cheese
½ cup	chopped parsley
½ Tsp.	salt
Dash	pepper
3 Tbsp.	bacon bits

Cook zucchini in boiling water until tender □ Cut ends off and slice them lengthwise in half □ Scoop out seeds and set aside □ Combine the rest of the ingredients and mix well □ Add ½ cup seeds to the mixture and stir in □ Fill each boat with cheese mixture and bake in Dutch oven for 10-15 minutes or until cheese melts and eggs set up.

FISH & POULTRY

ALMOND CHICKEN

(Serves 4-6) A Steven Shephard recipe.

1	chicken, cut up
1 cup	honey
1	6 oz. can concentrated orange juice
¼ cup	sherry
	Allspice, cinnamon, nutmeg, salt and pepper to taste
	Water — enough to obtain creamy texture
1 cup	sliced/chopped almonds

Lay chicken in Dutch oven □ Blend honey, orange juice, sherry and spices □ Add water to obtain creamy texture □ Pour sauce over chicken □ Sprinkle almonds on top.

Bake 1 hour with coals on top and bottom □ Serve over rice with sauce from oven.

BAKED WHEAT GERM CHICKEN

(Serves 4-6)

1	three-legged frying chicken
¼ lb.	butter, melted
1 cup	wheat germ
	Salt and pepper
	Paprika

Skin and dry the chicken pieces □ Roll in the melted butter and dip into the wheat germ, covering the entire piece of chicken □ Place in the bottom of a Dutch oven or in a baking dish □ When the whole chicken is coated, pour the remaining butter over it and salt and pepper □ Garnish with paprika and bake for 40-45 minutes in the Dutch oven and 45-50 minutes in a conventional oven at 350°F.

FISH AND POULTRY

CHICKEN AND ASPARAGUS CASSEROLE
(Serves 4-6)

1	3-lb. fryer, cut up
1½ Tsp.	salt
½ Tsp.	pepper
6 Tbsp.	butter
1	pkg. frozen, cut-up asparagus
2 Tbsp.	flour
1	can cream of mushroom soup
¼ cup	chicken broth
	Paprika

Sprinkle chicken with salt, pepper and paprika; brown in butter □ Place in Dutch oven or large casserole □ Stir in soup and broth □ Thaw and drain asparagus and stir into mixture, carefully □ Cover and bake at 375°F for 40-45 minutes or in the Dutch oven for 40 minutes.

CHICKEN ENCHILADAS
(Serves 6-8)

1	pkg. flour tortillas
2 lbs.	boned, cut-up chicken, cubed
1 pt.	sour cream
1 bunch	green onions, diced
1	8 oz. can tomato sauce
1	small can diced green chiles
1	can pitted black olives, chopped
1 lb.	jack cheese, shredded
½ lb.	cheddar cheese, shredded
2 Tbsp.	cumin
	Salt to taste

Brown chicken in Dutch oven and add onions; cook till onions are tenders; add chiles, olives, cumin and salt; mix well □ Fold in sour cream □ Cover the bottom of a Dutch oven with tortillas, put a layer of chicken mixture, cheese and tomato sauce; repeat this twice so you have 3 layers □ Cover the last layer with tortillas and sprinkle with cheese □ Bake 40-45 minutes and let stand 10 minutes before serving.

CRAB-STUFFED CHICKEN BREASTS
(Serves 8)

4	large chicken breasts, halved, skinned and boned
3 Tbsp.	butter or margarine
¼ cup	flour
¾ cup	milk
¾ cup	chicken broth
⅓ cup	dry white wine
¼ cup	chopped green onion
1 Tbsp.	butter or margarine
1	7½-oz. can crab meat
¼ lb.	fresh mushrooms, chopped
½ cup	wheat germ
2 Tbsp.	snipped parsley
½ Tsp.	salt
Dash	pepper
1 cup	shredded Swiss cheese
½ Tsp.	paprika

Place one chicken piece, boned side up, between 2 pieces of waxed paper □ Working from center out, pound chicken lightly with meat mallet to make cutlet about ⅛-inch thick □ Repeat with remaining chicken □ Set aside.

In saucepan, melt the 3 Tbsp. butter, blend in flour □ Add milk, chicken broth, and wine all at once; cook and stir till mixture thickens and bubbles □ Set aside □ Cook onion in the remaining butter till tender but not brown □ Stir in crab, mushrooms, wheat germ, parsley, salt and pepper □ Stir in 2 Tbsp. of the sauce □ Top each chicken piece with about ¼ cup crab mixture □ Fold sides in and roll up □ Place seam side down in Dutch oven □ Pour remaining sauce over all □ Bake, covered in 350°F oven for 1 hour or till chicken is tender, or in Dutch oven with coals top and bottom for 40-45 minutes □ Uncover and sprinkle with cheese and paprika □ Bake 2 minutes longer or till cheese melts.

COQ AU VIN
"chicken braised in wine" (6 servings)

2½ lb.	broiler-fryer, cut up (or 3 chicken breasts, halved, or 3 drumsticks and 3 thighs)
6	bacon slices, diced
⅔ cup	sliced green onions
8	small white onions, peeled
½ lb.	whole mushrooms
1	clove garlic, crushed
1 Tsp.	salt
¼ Tsp.	pepper
½ Tsp.	dried thyme leaves
8	small potatoes, scrubbed
2 cups	Burgundy
1 cup	chicken broth
	Chopped parsley

In Dutch oven or large skillet, saute diced bacon and green onions until bacon is crisp □ Remove and drain on paper towel □ Add chicken pieces to skillet and brown well on all sides □ Remove the chicken when it has browned and set aside □ Put peeled onions, mushrooms, and garlic in Dutch oven □ Add browned chicken pieces, bacon and green onions, salt, pepper, thyme, potatoes, wine, and chicken broth □ Cover and bake for 1 hour on medium heat.

FLORENTINED SOLE
(Serves 8-10)

3	pkg. frozen spinach (well drained)
4 lb.	sole filets
1 lb.	sour cream
¼ cup	chopped green onions
6	slices bacon
4 Tbsp.	fresh or dried parsley
	Salt and pepper

Combine spinach, half of sour cream, onions and mix well □ Spread the mixture on the bottom of the Dutch oven and place the filets on top □ Salt and pepper well □ Spread remainder of sour cream on filets and lay slices of bacon on top □ Sprinkle with parsley (and paprika, if desired) □ Bake 30 to 40 minutes.

MUSHROOM-STUFFED CHICKEN BREASTS WITH ARTICHOKES (Serves 6)

½ lb.	fresh mushrooms, sliced
6 Tbsp.	margarine
6-8	chicken breasts, boned and skinned
½ Tsp.	paprika
¼ Tsp.	pepper
1 pkg.	frozen artichoke hearts
2 Tbsp.	flour
⅔ cups	chicken broth
⅔ cup	dry sherry
	Salt to taste

Saute mushrooms in 2 Tbsp. margarine until browned □ Pound chicken breasts flat, boned side down on waxed paper □ Equally divide mushrooms in the center of each breast and roll up □ Add remaining margarine and brown in a large skillet or Dutch oven, placing the fold side down □ Sprinkle breasts with paprika and pepper □ Arrange breasts and artichokes in a Dutch oven or large, shallow baking dish □ Stir flour into margarine remaining in oven and gradually add stock and wine □ Bring to boil, stirring constantly □ Add salt to taste □ Pour sauce over chicken and artichokes □ Bake ¾ hour, basting occasionally □ Bake at 375°F for 1 hour in conventional oven.

POLLY BEMIS CHICKEN (Serves 4-6)

Polly Bemis, as a young Chinese woman, was sold as a slave and later was won in a poker game by Charles Bemis, who later married her. They moved down on the banks of the Salmon River in 1894, and Polly lived there till 1923. She was a hard worker, growing a productive garden, cutting firewood, cooking for Bemis, and caring for ducks, chickens, and a cow. Polly Creek on the Main Salmon River is named for her.

1	3 lb. cut-up chicken fryer
1 Tsp.	salt
1	8 oz. jar orange marmalade
1	bottle Russian dressing
1	fresh orange, thinly sliced

Brown chicken in bottom of Dutch oven □ Salt it well □ Pour over the marmalade and Russian dressing and arrange the fresh orange slices on top □ Bake 40-45 minutes.

SALMON CHEESE CASSEROLE
(Serves 4-6)

1	1 lb. can salmon (with liquid)
1	4 oz. can mushrooms, drained, or ¼ lb. fresh
1½ cups	bread crumbs
2	eggs, beaten
1 cup	grated cheddar cheese
1 Tbsp.	lemon juice
1 Tbsp.	minced onion

Flake fish in bowl, removing all bones □ Add all remaining ingredients and mix thoroughly in Dutch oven □ Bake 30-35 minutes.

SALMON SOUFFLE
(Serves 6)

3 Tbsp.	butter
3 Tbsp.	flour
1 Tsp.	salt
Dash	freshly ground pepper
1 cup	milk
1 can	1 lb. salmon, drained and flaked
2 Tbsp.	lemon juice
1 Tbsp.	grated onion
3 Tbsp.	chopped parsley
3	eggs, separated

Melt butter and blend in flour, salt and pepper □ Gradually add milk and cook, stirring until thickened □ Add next 4 ingredients □ Beat egg yolks until thick and lemon-colored and gradually stir into mixture □ Mix well, then gently fold in stiffly beaten egg whites □ Turn into buttered 1½-quart casserole or Dutch oven and bake in moderate oven (375°F) about 50 minutes or in the Dutch oven 35-40 minutes.

SCALLADOS
(Serves 6)

1 lb.	fresh or frozen scallops
3	medium avocados
	Lemon juice (fresh)
¼ cup	minced green onion
1 cup	fresh sliced mushrooms
½ Tsp.	salt
	Pepper
¾ cup	dry white wine
3 Tbsp.	margarine
4 Tbsp.	flour
¾ cup	milk
½ cup	grated Swiss cheese

Thaw scallops, if frozen □ Halve avocados lengthwise; remove seeds and peel halves □ Brush avocados with lemon juice; set aside □ Place the scallops in Dutch oven or saucepan with the wine, onion, mushrooms, salt and pepper □ Bring to a simmer, cover, and simmer very slowly for 5 minutes □ Remove scallops, mushrooms and onions to a bowl; put liquid aside in a cup.

Melt margarine in the Dutch oven and stir in the flour and cook slowly for 2 minutes without browning □ Remove from heat and beat in the scallop liquid slowly, stirring until sauce thickens □ Thin out with milk □ Carefully correct seasoning, adding lemon juice if needed.

Fold ⅔ of sauce into scallops and spoon into avocado halves □ Add cheese to remaining sauce and stir until cheese melts □ Spoon on the remaining sauce □ Refrigerate if not to be served immediately □ Reheat in covered Dutch oven to bubbling with heat on the top only □ In a conventional oven put under broiler until sauce is bubbling.

SEAFOOD THERMIDOR
(Serves 4)

If you think that lobster thermidor is the ultimate in good eating but you shudder at the cost, here's a delicious entree made with cod, the poor man's lobster.

1 lb.	fresh or frozen cod fillets
1	small onion, quartered
	Lemon slice
1 can	cream of shrimp soup
3 Tbsp.	flour
¼ cup	milk
¼ cup	dry white wine
¼ cup	shredded Mozzarella cheese
2 Tbsp.	snipped parsley
½ cup	soft bread crumbs
2 Tbsp.	grated Parmesan cheese
2 Tbsp.	margarine
½ Tsp.	paprika

Thaw fish; skin, if necessary □ Cut into ½-inch cubes □ Place fish, onion and lemon in greased skillet or Dutch oven □ Add water to cover □ Bring to boil; reduce heat and simmer, covered, 5-6 minutes, or until fish flakes easily.

In a small saucepan, blend soup and flour; gradually stir in milk and wine □ Cook and stir till thickened and bubbly □ Stir in the Mozzarella and parsley □ Heat through □ Carefully drain fish well; fold into sauce □ Spoon into scallop shells or onto plates □ Combine bread crumbs, Parmesan, margarine, and paprika □ Sprinkle over sauce □ Broil 1-2 minutes in conventional oven or in Dutch oven with heat on the top only, until the cheese melts.

SHRIMP QUICHE
(Serves 6-8)

	Pastry for a 10-inch pie shell
1 can	whole shrimp, well drained
⅓ cup	green onions, chopped (tops included)
3	eggs
1 cup	milk
½ Tsp.	salt
⅛ Tsp.	pepper
1 cup	Swiss cheese, shredded

Prepare the pastry from your own recipe or a pie crust mix for a 10-inch shell □ Line the bottom of the Dutch oven with pastry. Distribute shrimp over bottom of pastry shell □ Sprinkle evenly with onions and cheese □ Beat together the eggs, milk, salt and pepper □ Pour over shrimp and cheese □ Bake in 350°F oven for about 45 minutes or until custard is firm in center or in a Dutch oven for 35-40 minutes □ Let stand for 10 minutes before serving.

STICKY CHICKEN

My aunt, Mac Oliver, found this recipe in her local newspaper. She uses it to cook chunks of pheasant breasts, and it is a delicious variable.

1	chicken cut up
1	8 oz. jar apricot or pineapple jam
½ pkg.	Lipton onion soup (dry)
1	8 oz. jar French dressing (spicy)
	Salt and pepper

Mix the jam, dry soup and French dressing together and store in the refrigerator to enhance the flavor.

Cut up the chicken, place in Dutch oven and pour sauce over □ Salt and pepper to taste, cover and bake for 45 to 50 minutes or until tender.

THUNDER MOUNTAIN CHICKEN AND BROCCOLI
(Serves 6-8)

In 1900 Thunder Mountain was a gold mining boom area on Monumental Creek in the Salmon River Wilderness.

3 lbs.	boned chicken, cubed
1 bunch	fresh broccoli, cut into 2-inch pieces
2 cups	medium white sauce
2 Tbsp.	Beau Monde seasoning
½ Tsp.	salt
	Paprika

Prepare white sauce and add Beau Monde and salt; mix well □ Arrange chicken and broccoli in Dutch oven or casserole and pour sauce over the top □ Sprinkle with paprika and bake for 1 hour on moderate heat.

Medium White Sauce:

4 Tbsp.	butter or margarine
4 Tbsp.	flour
½ Tsp.	salt
2 cups	milk

Melt butter in saucepan over low heat □ Blend in flour, salt and dash pepper □ Add milk all at once □ Cook quickly, stirring constantly, till mixture thickens and bubbles □ Remove sauce from heat when it bubbles □ If sauce cooks too long, it becomes too thick and butter separates out □ To repair, stir in a little more milk □ Cook quickly, stirring constantly, till sauce bubbles □ A wooden spoon is handy for preparing sauces □ Use a heavy saucepan or Dutch oven.

TURKEY AND BROWN RICE CASSEROLE
(8 Servings)

3 cups	cooked turkey or chicken, left in large pieces
3½ cups	cooked brown rice
1 cup	chopped onion
1 cup	sliced celery
1 cup	chopped green pepper
3 Tbsp.	margarine
1 can	cream of mushroom soup
½ cup	dry white wine or chicken broth
1 can	sliced mushrooms, undrained
1 Tsp.	sage leaves, crumbled
½ Tsp.	salt
¼ Tsp.	thyme leaves
Dash	pepper
1 can	4 oz. pimientos drained and chopped
1 cup	herb-seasoned croutons

Combine turkey and rice in Dutch oven or 2½-qt. raised casserole; set aside □ Preheat oven to 350°F □ Preheat Dutch oven.

Saute onion, celery and green pepper in 2 Tbsp. margarine for 8 minutes, stirring frequently until tender-crisp □ Stir in soup, wine, mushrooms, sage, salt, thyme, pepper and pimientos.

Pour mushroom-vegetable mixture over turkey and rice in casserole or Dutch oven □ Stir with large spoon to combine □ Heat remaining 1 Tbsp. margarine until melted □ Toss croutons in melted margarine □ Spoon around edge of Dutch oven □ Bake 35-40 minutes with coals on top and bottom until bubbly □ Bake 40-45 minutes at 350°F in conventional oven.

DESSERTS

APPLE CRISP
(Serves 8-10) A Steven Shephard recipe.

Mix together:

3 cups	quick oats
2 cups	brown sugar
1 cup	flour
1 cup	butter
1 Tsp.	baking soda
2 Tsp.	salt
6-8	apples
2 Tsp.	cinnamon
2 Tsp.	nutmeg

Butter Dutch oven and cover bottom with half of crust mixture □ Mix thin sliced apples (6-8) with cinnamon and nutmeg □ Layer apples in oven about 2" thick over bottom crust □ Spread other half of crust mixture on top □ Bake 40 to 50 minutes with coals on top and bottom.

APPLESAUCE CAKE
(Serves 15)

1½ cups	honey
½ cup	margarine
2	eggs
2 Tsp.	soda
2½ cups	flour
½ Tsp.	allspice
1 Tsp.	cinnamon
1½ cups	applesauce
½ cup	boiling water

Mix all ingredients except water □ Add water after mixing well □ Mix and bake in Dutch oven 45-50 minutes.

BAKED APPLES

A Steven Shephard recipe.

Turn apples upside down and core from bottom to top without cutting completely through □ Fill apples with mixture of: raisins, honey, cinnamon, butter, and chopped nuts — Place apples in a greased pan that will fit inside of Dutch oven □ Pour water in pan to a depth of ½ inch □ Place pan on top of pebbles in bottom of Dutch oven □ Bake for 20 minutes, top and bottom.

CAMEL GULCH CARROT CAKE
(Serves 10-12)

Camel Gulch is a drainage about 182 miles down the Salmon River in Idaho, named for the John Camel family that lived at the mouth in the early days.

3 cups	flour
1½ Tsp.	baking soda
1½ Tsp.	baking powder
2 Tsp.	cinnamon
3 cups	sugar
4 cups	oil
6	eggs
4½ cups	grated carrots
¾ cup	walnuts, chopped

Mix together the first five ingredients □ Add the oil and blend; add the eggs one at a time and beat after each addition □ Add the carrots and walnuts, blend well and pour into lightly buttered Dutch oven □ Bake 20-25 minutes □ Let cool and frost with Cream Cheese Frosting which follows:

Cream Cheese Frosting:

1 pkg.	cream cheese (8 oz.), softened
1 cup	confectioner's sugar
2 Tsp.	vanilla
¼ cup	milk

Combine the above ingredients and beat until fluffy and smooth.

CHERRY PIE

Prepare your favorite pastry for a 10-inch shell.

3 cups	pitted, fresh, ripe, tart red cherries
1 cup	sugar
¼ cup	flour
dash	salt
2 Tbsp.	butter

Line the bottom of the Dutch oven with the pastry or put the pie tin directly in the bottom of the Dutch oven □ Combine cherries, sugar, flour and salt □ Turn into Dutch oven and dot with butter □ Adjust lattice top with the rest of the pastry; seal □ Bake for 40-45 minutes □ Let cool before slicing.

GLAZED PEACH PIE
(Serves 8)

1	10-inch Dutch oven or one 9-inch pie tin*
5 cups	sliced fresh peaches
¾ cup	fructose (or granulated sugar)
3 Tbsp.	flour
½ Tsp.	nutmeg
¼ Tsp.	salt
1 Tsp.	lemon juice
¼ Tsp.	almond extract
¼ cup	apricot preserves (in jar)

Make pie shell with high edges, from favorite recipe or piecrust mix; preheat oven to 425°F or heat lid to Dutch oven.

Toss together peaches, sugar, flour, nutmeg, salt, lemon juice, almond extract □ Over bottom of pie shell arrange 2 circles of peach slices, all pointing to center; top with 2 more layers of peach slices, arranged in same way.

Bake pie 15-20 minutes, then cover with foil and bake 15 to 20 minutes longer until peaches are fork-tender □ Melt apricot preserves, then use to brush over top of peaches □ Cool pie.

*The pie dough can be put directly into the bottom of the Dutch oven or put in a pie tin and then into the Dutch oven to bake.

RUBY RAPID RHUBARB
(Serves 8-10)

This is a recipe from my mother, Jane McDonald, adapted to a Dutch oven and renamed on the Main Salmon River.

Crust:

1 cup	flour
⅓ cup	powdered sugar
½ cup	margarine

Mix and press into bottom of heated Dutch oven □ Bake 15 minutes, being careful not to burn the bottom.

2	eggs beaten
1½ cup	sugar
¼ cup	flour
¾ tsp.	salt
2 cups	finely chopped rhubarb

Spread on top of the crust and bake ½ hour □ Let stand 15 minutes before serving.

STRAWBERRY YOGURT CHEESECAKE
(Serves 8)

Crust:

1	10-inch metal pie tin (glass if baked in conventional oven)
1 pkg.	graham crackers, crushed
¼ cup	honey
¼ lb.	melted margarine

2 cups	plain yogurt
1	8 oz. pkg. cream cheese
¼ cup.	honey
¼ Tsp.	salt
2	eggs
2 Tsp.	vanilla
1	large carton fresh strawberries

Melt margarine and honey together and mix with crackers □ Press crust firmly into pie tin □ Let cream cheese soften; beat with vanilla until creamy □ Add the yogurt, honey, salt and mix well □ Add eggs one at a time mixing just until blended □ Pour mixture into shell and bake about one hour, or until firm □ Let cool and top with sliced strawberries □ Chill at least one hour.

STREUSELY BAKED APPLES
(Serves 3-6)

12	pitted dates
3	large apples, cored and halved
½ cup	sugar
½ cup	flour
¼ Tsp.	ground cinnamon and cardamom
3 Tbsp.	butter
1 cup	light cream

Place 2 dates in hollow of each apple half □ Stir together the sugar, flour, cinnamon and cardamom; add butter and rub mixture between fingers until butter lumps are no longer there □ Divide mixture equally between 6 apple halves □ Using your fingers, pack mixture tightly in a mound over each □ Bake, uncovered, in a 250°F oven for 30 minutes or in a Dutch oven with coals on top and bottom for 15-20 minutes, or until apples are tender when pierced □ Pass light cream to serve with fruit.

SUE'S APPLE RAISIN CRUMBLE

This recipe was given to me by a good friend, Bill Caccia, who borrowed it from an Australian friend. He uses his Dutch oven on his old Majestic cook stove at home, as well as over a campfire on float trips.

Core and slice 6 large apples □ Place them in the Dutch oven □ Add ½ cup raisins □ Pour ½ cup honey over mixture and sprinkle with cinnamon.

Make a crumble mixture out of the following: (Can be premixed to take on a river trip or camping)

1½ cups	quick oats, uncooked
1 Tbsp.	sesame seeds
1 Tbsp.	wheat germ
¼ cup	coconut
¼ cup	sunflower seeds

Cut in ½ cup margarine □ Add a bit of honey to get the mixture crumbly □ Cover the apples and raisins with the crumble and bake for 30 minutes or until top is golden brown □ Bake at 350° in conventional oven.

DESSERTS

SUGARLESS APPLE TARTS
(Serves 12)

1 can	frozen apple juice concentrate (12 oz.)
2 Tbsp.	butter
3 Tbsp.	quick-cooking tapioca
⅛ Tsp.	salt
1 Tsp.	ground cinnamon
½ Tsp.	ground nutmeg
6-7 cups	peeled, thinly sliced Golden Delicious apples
	Pastry for a 9-inch double-crust pie
½ cup	chopped walnuts (optional)

In Dutch oven combine apple juice, butter, tapioca, salt, cinnamon, nutmeg and apples □ Simmer, covered, stirring gently occasionally, until apples are tender when pierced, about 10-15 minutes □ Cool, cover and chill up to 4 days.

Prepare your favorite pastry □ On a floured board roll out pastry to about ⅛-inch thick □ Cut into twelve 4½-inch rounds □ Drape pastry rounds over the backs of 2½-inch muffin cups, alternating cups so pastry does not touch* □ Shape dough around cup □ Prick bottom of each round □ Bake for 5-7 minutes or until golden brown in Dutch oven or at 450°F in your conventional oven □ Let cool before removing from pan or Dutch □ Spoon about ⅓ cup apple filling into each tart shell □ Garnish each with sweetened whipped cream, if desired, and nuts.

*If using a Dutch oven, you will need to use a round muffin tin or individual aluminum muffin cups.

YOGURT CHOCOLATE CAKE

In saucepan or Dutch oven, combine 1 slightly beaten egg, ⅔ cup sugar, ½ cup milk, and three 1-oz. squares unsweetened chocolate □ Cook and stir over medium heat till chocolate melts and mixture comes just to boiling; cool □ Cream 1 cup sugar and ½ cup shortening till light □ Add 1 Tsp. vanilla and 2 eggs, one at a time, beating well after each □ Sift together 2 cups sifted cake flour, 1 Tsp. soda, and ½ Tsp. salt □ Add to creamed mixture alternately with 1 cup plain or fruit yogurt, beating after each addition □ Blend in chocolate mixture □ Bake in greased and floured Dutch oven or cake pan □ In the Dutch oven bake 20 to 25 minutes; in the conventional oven bake at 350°F for 25-30 minutes □ Let cool and frost with your favorite frosting or sprinkle with powdered sugar.

When you are camping you may want to use a cake mix and substitute the yogurt for the water. It makes a very moist cake.

APPENDIX

BUILDING A FIRE

There is more to building a fire outdoors than meets the eye. In this era of overpopulation and the clamor for the last of living and breathing space, open fires are not welcome and are often prohibited, especially in forested or grassland areas. The cutting of standing trees is forbidden practically everywhere, and with good reason.

Select a place for your fire very carefully. A spot protected from the wind, not too close to trees, near water, and on solid soil. An ideal fire-building method is through the use of a fire pan, large enough so that the ashes and coals are easily contained, and of strong enough metal so that the fire will not burn through it. Garbage can lids are not sufficient. A sheet-metal firepan with three-inch sides is ideal. Such pans are readily available from any sheet metal shop or from some river supply catalogs. To save space they can be made to fit the bottom of your cooler or used as a tray for your grate. This makes it possible, if you are camping in the wilderness, to pack all your ashes out with you. Using a firepan also discourages the building of a "white man's fire," a large and wasteful bonfire.

Charcoal briquets are readily available at your local grocery store and are the desired heat source for Dutch oven cooking. Otherwise, select hardwoods, if possible, from **dead** timber. The kind of firewood used has a great deal to do with the quality of outdoor cooking and cooking time. This, however, can be determined only through individual experience; not through a cookbook.

Softwoods burn too quickly. Some woods pop and crackle, some smoke and leave hot embers, and others burn down to small ash.

Cooking fires should be no larger than necessary to do the job, and actual cooking should not begin until the fire has burned down to glowing coals. Remember to throw your matches into the fire after using them and not on the ground. Another tip on keeping the campgrounds and wilderness clean is to go prepared to carry out all your garbage and never bury it.

WHERE TO BUY A CAMP DUTCH OVEN

Aluminum Dutch ovens can be purchased from the
following sources in ten- and twelve-inch sizes:

American River Supplies
P.O. Box 2524
Idaho Falls, Idaho   83401

Scott Manufacturing Company
2525 Monroe Avenue
Cleveland, Ohio 44113

The cast-iron models are often available in your local
hardware and sporting goods stores. One manufacturer
is:

The Atlanta Stove Works, Inc.
P.O. Box 5254
Atlanta, Georgia   30307

A FORK IN THE TRAIL

It is the little things gained from years of trial and error experience, or from many diverse cookbooks, that led to delicious food coming from our kitchen. Based on Sheila's knowledge of nutrition, she has taken our family down the path marked "Well balanced diet," to a condition best described as happiness through wellness. I hope this book will help lead you down the same path.

Sheila earned a degree in Consumer Economics from the University of Montana at Missoula. From that basis in college, she began studying nutrition, realizing the need for a balanced diet that leads to well-being and personal happiness. Though this book's theme is delicious main course meals, Sheila's left it up to you to create a complete meal.

David Mills

CREDITS

Editorial/Creative Direction
Colleen Allen

Design
David E. Canaan Design

Illustrations
Parry Merkley

Photography
Doug Martin

Lithography
Press Publishing Ltd.

INDEX